HORRIBLE HISTORIES

ANNUAL 2011

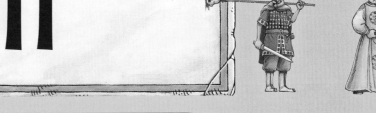

This book belongs to:

_____

_____

SCHOLASTIC

Contents

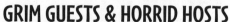

Stone Age Funerals

What's the spookiest place you can think of? (Apart from an empty staff room.) How about the very first burial places of all? Our Stone Age ancestors had some eerie and odd ideas about the dead...

Before they buried people, Stone-Agers had to release the spirit from the dead body it was trapped in. And the spirit could only leave when the flesh had rotted away and was falling off the bones. To speed things up they might hack the flesh off with a stone knife. If they weren't in a rush, they would leave Grandpa outside for the animals and birds to pick clean. (Maybe they had a bone to pick with him!)

BUT I'M NOT DEAD!

PERHAPS... BUT YOU'RE NOT VERY WELL

Buried presents

Once the dead were thoroughly bony, the Stone-Agers would then bury their loved ones with...

• **Flowers.** It seems that Neanderthals (Homo sapiens sapiens' extinct cousins) did flower arranging! Several types of flowers were found in a bunch in a Stone Age grave in Iraq.

SNIFF
WILT

• **Necklaces of animal teeth**. Jewellery helped Stone Age spooks look smart as they wafted around the afterlife.

SO THAT'S WHAT HAPPENED TO MY BEST LION'S TOOTH NECKLACE

OOOOOOH

FUNERAL STEW

There's a surprising number of Stone Age burial sites scattered across the British Isles. On Anglesey in Wales there's a stone burial chamber called Barclodiad y Gawres. Archaeologists have worked out the revolting ritual that went on at the funeral of two boys...

• Their bodies were cremated till the flesh burned off.

BURN BURN BURN

BARBECUED...

• The bones were scraped, mixed with sheep bones and buried under a layer of earth.

SCRAPE SCRAPE SCRAPE

SPARE, RIBS...

• Inside the chamber, a fire was lit under a water pot.

BOIL BOIL

AND A BOILED POT

A stew was stirred into the water... made from oysters, limpets, winkles, eels, frogs, toads, grass snakes, mice and shrews. If it crawled, crept or squeaked, it went in. After a good bit of boiling and bubbling, the shells, bones, snake skins and mouse guts were strained out and the soup was drunk. Delicious. (Sounds almost as bad as a school dinner oxtail and vegetable soup.)

Bony Barrow

West Kennet Long Barrow is a spooky mound in Wiltshire. It's where late-Stone Age locals buried the bones of their dead.

Skulls and bones were placed with great care inside the dark barrow.

Many of the skeletons were buried with bits missing. This may have been because wild animals nicked bones to nibble while the bodies were lying around waiting to be buried.

Another blood-chilling barrow can be seen on the horizon.

The bones of just a few special people were buried here, so each burial was an eerily important occasion. It was carried out by local holy men or women, and they would have dressed up specially for the ceremony.

YOU CAN HAVE MY RIBS, BUT LEAVE MY TOE BONES ALONE – I'M TICKLISH

Dead bodies were left on special platforms outside the barrow to rot until they were little more than bones. The flesh may also have been scraped off the skeletons with sharp stone blades.

Terrify Your Teacher

Test your teacher to see if they have Neanderthal knowledge... or just look the part.

TEACHER

NEANDERTHAL

1. Stone-Agers made paint by mixing powdered minerals with a liquid. But what liquid?

a) Mammoth pee
b) Gooseberry beer
c) Blood

2. What did Stone-Agers use as toilet paper?

a) Moss
b) Deer skin
c) Hedgehog skin

3. How did Bolivian Stone-Agers keep their spare spuds fresh?

a) By burying them in a potato pit
b) By frying them in llama fat so they turned into crisps
c) By sprinkling them with water and leaving them out at night so they froze

4. What did some clean Stone-Agers do that even modern humans forget?

a) Cleaned their teeth
b) Polished their shoes
c) Washed up after dinner

5. How did Stone-Agers celebrate special occasions?

a) By setting off fireworks

b) By drinking lots of booze

c) By wrestling with cave bears

Answers on page 60.

Home Horrors

Tens of thousands of years later, the Celts – a people from central Europe who made themselves at home in the British Isles – made their own homes and holy places scarier than their graves!

Terrible Trophies

After battle, the Celts had the charming habit of cutting off the heads of the enemies they'd killed. Roman writers said the Celts fastened the heads on to the chariots. The dead heads were taken home and nailed up over the warrior's front door to show the neighbours what a hero he was. Old heads were preserved in cedar oil and brought out now and again when the warrior fancied a bit of a boast. Some would boast that they refused to part with their enemy's heads, even though they'd been offered the head's weight in gold. But it wasn't just the heads they kept...

Foul Facts

Here's a warrior trophy that takes a lot of brains. To make it you will need a sharp sword, a wooden spoon, and some lime (or cement).

1. Pick a fight with another hero. The fiercer he is, the greater the glory.

2. Kill him. (If he kills you, stop reading here.)

3. Remove his head.

4. Remove the brain from the skull.

5. Mix the brain with lime to make a hard round ball.

6. Show your prize at feasts and boast about your bravery.

9

Fireside Frights

Welcome to a Celt party! Tonight's entertainment is a quiz. Get all the questions right and you'll fit in well. Get one wrong and things might turn nasty. You'll end up with something at your throat. If you're lucky it might be a slave chain – if you're unlucky it might be a Druid's knife!

1. The wine or beer is passed around. As a special guest you have to drink first. But how should you do it?
a) Empty your goblet in one gulp.
b) Refuse to drink until the chief has drunk first.
c) Drink a sip then pass it on.

2. As the party goes on, a warrior stands up and tells everyone how he bravely fought against ten Roman soldiers and beat all of them. Everyone looks at you. What do you say?
a) "Liar! Liar! Pants on fire!"
b) "You are a brave and noble warrior. I believe you and praise your courage."
c) "That's nothing mate! I beat 20 Roman soldiers – I had one hand tied behind my back, I was wearing a blindfold and my only weapon was a sharp fingernail."

3. A wild boar has been roasted. You are offered a trotter to chew on. What do you say?
a) "Thank you – that is extremely kind of you."
b) "I hope you've checked this boar for mad pig disease! Anyway I'm a vegetarian."
c) "I will eat nothing but the best meat. Give me the finest flesh or you will die and I'll be roasting you on the fire."

4. The Druid is a kind old bloke in a long hooded robe. He says he has a special drink for a noble guest like you. It is made from the juice of the mistletoe. What do you do?
a) Drink it.
b) Offer to share it with the Druid.
c) Refuse to drink it. Make some excuse, like you were always taught to say "No!" to a stranger… and they don't come much stranger than the Druid!

Riddle Muddle

On dark winter nights the Celts had no television to keep themselves amused. They were very fond of riddles, though. Can you be a Celtic clever clogs and solve this one?
Clue: 'one leg' could 'meat' with a pet…

IN COME TWO LEGS CARRYING ONE LEG, LAY DOWN ONE LEG ON THREE LEGS, OUT GO TWO LEGS, IN COME FOUR LEGS, OUT GO FIVE LEGS, IN COME TWO LEGS, SNATCHES UP THREE LEGS, FLINGS IT AT FOUR LEGS AND BRINGS BACK ONE LEG.

Rude as a Royal

Royals can be as rude as a big brother. (Imagine no one could ever tell you off. How naughty would YOU try to be?!) Some kings and queens were majestically messy and rude. Here's how to match a misbehaving monarch's manners.

Pick your nose in public
Don't worry, this is what James I did. (But remember it is only polite to lick your finger before shaking hands with someone.)

Spit often and in large quantities
William IV did this. Some people said he was not a gentleman. But he had been in the navy a long time and, like other sailors, was used to spitting into the sea (where the fish probably objected – but why should he worry? He wasn't the Prince of Whales, was he?).

Be a messy eater
James I was the messiest monarch. Visitors said his tongue was too big for his mouth, which made him spill his drink from each side of his mouth.

Throw bones to the dog
Henry VIII did and he never had a hungry dog. (Don't throw bones to the servants. Bread and water is enough for them.)

Wear two pairs of trousers
When James I wore holes in his trousers, he didn't throw them away or even change them. He simply slipped another pair over the top of them.

Take a bath – four times a year
Elizabeth I washed just four times a year. John was a bit better. He had two baths a month. But he was still smelly. His nickname was 'Lackland' but perhaps it should've been 'Lack-Friends'?

Snore loudly
Henry I snored very, very loudly to let his family know that he hadn't died in his sleep. So don't worry. The others in the palace won't get any sleep but the lower classes don't need as much sleep as a monarch. Anyway, they should be awake to guard you.

Not-So-Gorgeous Georges

Few British kings were so consistently selfish and silly as these fanciful fellas called George, who ruled from the 18th to the early 19th century. Meet the gang...

GEORGE I GEORGE II GEORGE III GEORGE IV

Gorging number four

George IV was one of the laziest and vainest kings in British history; vain enough to cover his face in chalk dust and use leeches to suck his blood – just to look pale! He loved food, fashion and girlfriends. That nursery rhyme 'Georgie Porgie'? It's about our fat friend. And he really did 'kiss the girls and make them cry'.

The behaviour of these Georges was enough to make even the most powder-puffed Georgian blush in embarrassment.

Number two's tantrums

George II was famous for his temper tantrums. He'd stamp about, shake his fists and kick his wig around the room if he didn't get his way.

George hated England. He said all the men talked about was boring politics, and all the women talked about was clothes. (Maybe he had a point?!)

Cash for a queen

George IV married one of his girlfriends, Maria Fitzherbert, in secret. (Maria wasn't keen, but George said he'd stab himself if she didn't, so she gave in.)

The trouble was, Maria was a Catholic, and Parliament didn't want a Catholic queen. They offered to pay all of greedy George's debts – if he dumped Maria and married his cousin Caroline instead. And guess what?

THE MONEY – OR YOUR WIFE?

George took the cash and Caroline – even though she was podgy and rarely washed her knickers. (Sounds like the perfect match!)

DID YOU KNOW?

George II was the last British king to lead his troops in battle. But when he charged the enemy, his horse galloped off in the other direction – with the royal grumpster clinging on to the reins for dear life.

Royal Rumpus

German George I was a lazy spud, George II took a Jaco-bite out of the Scots, George III went barmy, and Georgie-porgie IV ate all the pies. These kings were pretty bad – and their subjects were revolting. What a load of Georgian argy-bargy!

WHEN BRITAIN'S STUART QUEEN, ANNE, DIED IN 1714, THE BRITS HAD A PROBLEM. ANNE HAD BEEN A PROTESTANT – BUT ALL HER HEIRS WERE CATHOLICS.

WE DON'T WANT ONE OF THESE CATHOLICS RULING US, DO WE?

WHY DON'T WE ASK GEORGE OF HANOVER TO BE OUR KING? HE'S NOT A CATHOLIC

HEY, GOOD IDEA!

GERMAN GEORGE TOOK THE JOB AND WAS CROWNED KING GEORGE I OF ENGLAND. NEVER MIND THAT HE WAS A LAZY COUCH POTATO AND DIDN'T EVEN SPEAK ENGLISH!

OH WELL, AT LEAST HE ISN'T A CATHOLIC!

OF COURSE, NOT EVERYBODY WAS PLEASED WITH THE NEW GERMAN KING. UP IN SCOTLAND, JAMES EDWARD STUART TRIED TO START A REBELLION (THE JACOBITE* UPRISING) AGAINST GEORGIE. HIS REBELS GOT CRUSHED BY GEORGE'S ARMY.

UH OH!

CHOP 'EM INTO JACO –BITS!

*'JACOBUS' IS POSH FOR 'JAMES' – SO HIS SUPPORTERS WERE JACOBITES.

GEORGE I WASN'T POPULAR. EVEN HIS SON GEORGE II WAS GLAD WHEN HE DIED...

YOUR DAD'S DEAD. HERE'S THE CROWN.

YESSSS!!

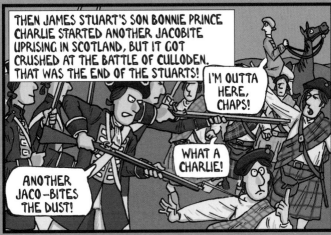

THEN JAMES STUART'S SON BONNIE PRINCE CHARLIE STARTED ANOTHER JACOBITE UPRISING IN SCOTLAND, BUT IT GOT CRUSHED AT THE BATTLE OF CULLODEN. THAT WAS THE END OF THE STUARTS!

I'M OUTTA HERE, CHAPS!

WHAT A CHARLIE!

ANOTHER JACO –BITES THE DUST!

TEN YEARS LATER IT WAS THE END FOR GEORGE II, TOO. WHEN HE DIED HIS GRANDSON GEORGE III TOOK OVER.

IN THE COUNTRYSIDE, RICH FARMERS WERE KICKING POOR FARMERS OFF THEIR LAND TO SET UP BIGGER FARMS. THIS WAS CALLED 'ENCLOSURE'.

YOU'D BETTER GET WEAVING...

WHAT CAN WE DO NOW?

AND RICH FACTORY OWNERS WERE BUILDING MILLS WITH NEWLY INVENTED STEAM-POWERED WEAVING MACHINES - WHICH PUT LOTS OF POOR WEAVERS OUT OF WORK.

MY MACHINES DO THE WORK OF A HUNDRED MEN!

GRRR!

WEAVING MILL

A LOT OF POOR PEOPLE GOT VERY UPSET. THERE WERE RIOTS WHEN OUT-OF-WORK WEAVERS BROKE INTO FACTORIES AND SMASHED UP WEAVING MACHINES. SOME EVEN DRESSED UP AS WOMEN SO THEY COULD SNEAK IN AND GET SMASHING!

HELP! SOME REALLY UGLY WOMEN ARE SMASHING MY MACHINES!

DRAT! I'VE GOT A LADDER IN MY TIGHTS!

A LOT OF POOR PEOPLE HAD TO TURN TO CRIME TO SURVIVE - LIKE THE FOUL BUT FAMOUS HIGHWAYMAN, DICK TURPIN.

YOUR MONEY OR MY LIFE... WAIT, THAT'S NOT RIGHT

WHAT A TURNIP

IN BRITAIN'S AMERICAN COLONIES, THE SETTLERS WERE SICK OF BEING BOSSED AROUND BY THE BRITS. IN BOSTON IN 1773 THEY REBELLED BY DRESSING UP AS INDIANS AND THROWING LOADS OF TEA SHIPPED FROM BRITAIN INTO THE HARBOUR.

THERE'S TROUBLE BREWING!

IN 1775 THE AMERICANS STARTED A WAR OF INDEPENDENCE AGAINST BRITAIN. IN 1783 THE AMERICANS FINALLY WON AND FOUNDED THEIR OWN COUNTRY - THE USA!

EXCEPT INDIANS...

AND SLAVES...

AND ANYONE ELSE WE DON'T LIKE

WE'RE SICK OF KINGS! WE'LL START A COUNTRY WHERE EVERYONE'S EQUAL

IN THIS TIME OF RIOTS AND REVOLUTIONS, BRITAIN NEEDED A STRONG, SMART KING. UNFORTUNATELY, GEORGE III WENT BONKERS! HIS FAT, GREEDY SON GEORGE WAS MADE PRINCE REGENT SO HE COULD FILL IN FOR HIS MAD DAD.

BOIL MY SHRIMPS, VICAR! PEACOCK!

THERE'S A RIOT IN MANCHESTER, YOUR MAJESTY!

YOUR DAD'S GOT A LOT ON HIS MIND – WOULD YOU MIND STEPPING IN?

OKAY

OVER THE CHANNEL IN FRANCE, THE PEASANTS WERE ALSO SICK OF BEING PUSHED AROUND BY THEIR KING AND HIS NOBLES. THEY HAD A REVOLUTION, AND THE HIGH AND MIGHTY FRENCH KING LOUIS LOST HIS HEAD.

HOORAY!

KING LOUIS USED TO BE A LOT HIGHER!

CHARGE!

IN THE MESS THAT FOLLOWED, A BLOKE CALLED NAPOLEON TOOK OVER IN FRANCE, AND DECLARED WAR ON JUST ABOUT EVERYONE IN EUROPE (INCLUDING BRITAIN!). THE WAR LASTED ALMOST TWENTY YEARS.

HMM... SO THE FRENCH LEADER IS THE GREATEST GENERAL IN THE WORLD – AND ALL WE'VE GOT IS A MAD KING?

THE BRITISH AND THEIR ALLIES, LED BY THE DUKE OF WELLINGTON, FINALLY BEAT NAPOLEON AT WATERLOO.

WELLINGTON REALLY GAVE THE FRENCH THE BOOT!

WHEN MAD OLD GEORGE DIED HIS GREEDY SON (NOW KING GEORGE IV) SAW IT AS A CHANCE TO LIVE LARGE.

YOUR DAD'S DEAD, YOUR MAJESTY.

my new palace!

EXCELLENT! I'LL HAVE TWO CURRIED TURTLES, A DOZEN CREAM CAKES AND A BARREL OF FRENCH WINE TO CELEBRATE!

GEORGIE'S GREEDINESS DID FOR HIM IN THE END, THOUGH. HE DIED FROM OVEREATING.

YES, HE HASN'T FINISHED HIS PUDDING!

SOMETHING MUST BE WRONG WITH HIM

URGLE!

GEORGE'S DEATH BROUGHT THE GHASTLY GEORGIAN ERA TO AN END. GEORGIE FOUR'S SAILOR UNCLE WILLIAM BECAME KING, BUT HE SOON DIED – AND A TEENAGE GIRL CALLED VICTORIA BECAME QUEEN. BUT THAT'S ANOTHER STORY...

Royal Rotters... and Rats!

It will take all your Horrible Histories knowledge to name these 29 misbehaving monarchs! Their names are at the bottom of the page – in the wrong order, of course.
Oh, and six rodents have crept in – can you spot them all?

ELIZABETH I	WILLIAM III	WILLIAM THE CONQUEROR	EDWARD THE CONFESSOR
JOHN	HENRY IV	ELIZABETH II	MARY I
HENRY V	CHARLES I	GEORGE III	EDWARD VII
EDWARD VI	EDWARD V	RICHARD THE LIONHEART	HENRY I
STEPHEN	HAROLD	WILLIAM IV	EDWARD II
VICTORIA	JAMES I	JAMES II	HENRY VI
RICHARD III	HENRY VIII	MARY I	CHARLES II
MATILDA			

20

Greedy Edward

Son of Queen Victoria, Edward VII was a particularly amusing monarch... if you find eating and shooting funny.

Albert Edward Saxe-Coburg – Edward VII to you – was often rather rude and amusing with his food…

• One night at a posh dinner, the King dropped a speck of spinach on to his white shirt. So he roared, plunged his hands into the spinach and smeared the rest of it all over his fat chest!

• When a footman accidentally spilled cream down Ed's front, Ed spluttered, "My good man, I am not a strawberry!" Mind you, he was… a potato! The famous King Edward spud was named after him.

• Ed was once eating and talking away when his grandson cried, "Grandpa!" He was told not to interrupt. "When I've finished speaking you'll be allowed to say what you want to," the King said.

Finally, he turned to his grandson and said, "Now I've finished. What was it you wanted to say?" "I was going to tell you there was a caterpillar on your lettuce," the child replied. "It's all right now – you've eaten it."

DAFT DEEDS

Edward was once riding in a carriage with his nephew, Kaiser Wilhelm II of Germany. They didn't really like each other but they chatted and tried to be polite. Suddenly one of the horses farted. The pong filled the carriage. Both monarchs ignored it... but then it happened again! Embarrassed, Edward apologised. The Kaiser replied...

MY DEAR UNCLE BERTIE, PLEASE DON'T MENTION IT – I REALLY THOUGHT IT WAS ONE OF THE HORSES

BIG EDDIE'S CELEBRITY FAT CLUB

Fancy getting into the same shape as Edward himself? Then try this awfully unhealthy regime!

DIET

Five large meals a day. Make sure they are BIG — some more than tencourses.

SMOKING

Smoke lots. At least twelve cigars and twenty cigarettes every day.

EXERCISE

Hunting or driving. Anything as long as it involves sitting down while something else does the work!

HORRIBLE HISTORIES HEALTH WARNING:

DON'T FOLLOW THIS REGIME — it could kill you.
Big Eddie died of bronchial asthma in 1910. The cigars couldn't have helped!

Awful for Animals

England is supposed to be a nation of animal lovers,
isn't it? Not if you're a monkey, a dog or a bull!

The English are famous for loving animals. But that's not the whole picture. England has never been a happy home for animals. It's always been…

Miserable for monkeys

In the 1830s Jack Mytton was a rich (but stupid) Englishman. One of his favourite pets was a monkey that went out hunting on horseback with him. Mutt-head Mytton decided it would be a funny trick to teach his monkey to drink wine. The monkey enjoyed it and got a taste for it, but one day, desperate for a drink, he drank a bottle of boot polish… and it polished him off.

THAT'S SHOE-BOOZE, FOLKS!

CRUMP

Deadly for dogs

The English love dogs. Don't they? Er.... no. When the First World War started, any German type of dog could be treated with terrible cruelty because England was at war with Germany. Dachshunds were kicked in the street and two were burned alive. German Shepherd dogs were re-named 'Alsatians' to protect them!

DID YOU KNOW?

The phrase 'raining cats and dogs' comes from England in the 1600s. During heavy downpours of rain, mangy street moggies and soggy road doggies drowned. It looked as if their bodies had fallen with the rain.

BRUTAL FOR BULLS

The English never went in for bullfighting, but they did enjoy setting their dogs to fight bulls in the 1700s and 1800s. Butchers barmily said that the beef tasted better if a bull was angry when it was killed. And making the bull furious with dogs turned into the 'sport'. It also led to the ancient Horrible Histories joke....

WAS THIS BULL MAD?
WELL, HE WASN'T VERY PLEASED

The aim was for the dog to grab the bull by the nose and hang on.
• The bull was tied up and a dog let into the ring.
• If the dog failed it could be tossed to death on the bull's horns.
• Another dog would be sent into the ring... and another.
• If a dog 'won' then the bull was killed. This 'sport' was finally banned in 1835. Why? Was it because...
a) young Princess Victoria said it was cruel?
b) men at bullrings got drunk and had fights?
c) England was running out of bulls?
Answer on page 60.

Beastly for French beasts

Of course, the English aren't alone in being awful to animals. You have probably heard jokes about the fact that the French have been known to eat frogs' legs.

THE CHEF TOLD ME MY LEGS LOOKED LOVELY...

Well, in France, it wasn't just amphibians who had a lot to fear. Porkers were prosecuted and swans got worn out, too.

Shocking for *les chiens*

In the 1370s the villainous Charles of Navarre had an argument with the Count of Foix about some money. Charles gave the count's son a bag of powder. "Feed this magic powder to your father and we'll be friends again." The Count of Foix found the powder and fed it to his dogs instead. The dogs howled in agony and died… cos the powder was poison. Some dogs were luckier – Henry III used to carry a basket of small doggy pets with him. They were hung around his neck.

SMALL DOGGY PETS

Poor pigs

In Dijon in the Middle Ages pigs wandered the streets looking for scraps of food. It was a hard life so the pigs were tough. One pig ate a young child. The pig was put on trial for murder and was found guilty. Murderers in France were hanged – so the good people of Dijon hanged the pig.

In 1740 a cow was hanged. Her crime? She was found guilty of being a witch. How udder-ly crazy.

WHAT'S THE CHURCH'S POSITION ON EATING MURDERERS?

SUFFERING SWANS

In the Middle Ages the French had a sport for July and August each year – swan catching. This was a chance for everyone, from the nobles and the churchmen to the peasants, to join together in tormenting young swans.

It was important, of course, that you went after swans that were too young to fly away…

CHOOSE A POND OR CANAL WHERE THERE ARE LOTS OF YOUNG SWANS.

TEAMS HAVE A BOAT EACH AND SET OFF IN ORDER – PRIESTS FIRST, LORDS SECOND AND PEASANTS THIRD.

LIGHT YOUR WAY WITH FLAMING TORCHES AND HAVE LOTS OF LOUD MUSIC. CHASE THE YOUNG SWANS.

THE TEAM THAT CATCHES THE MOST SWANS IS THE WINNER. YOU ARE NOT ALLOWED TO KILL THE SWANS – JUST SCARE THE FEATHERS OFF THEM.

KEEP GOING FOR SEVERAL DAYS, WITH BREAKS FOR PARTIES, TILL YOU – AND THE SWANS – ARE EXHAUSTED.

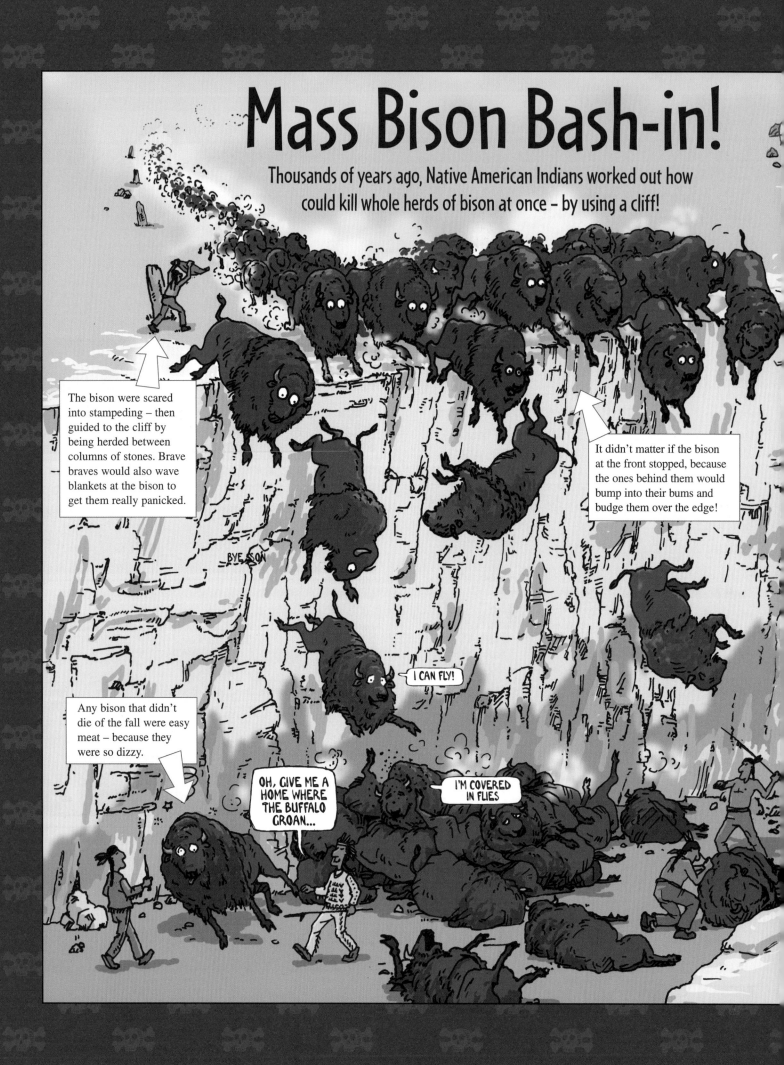

28

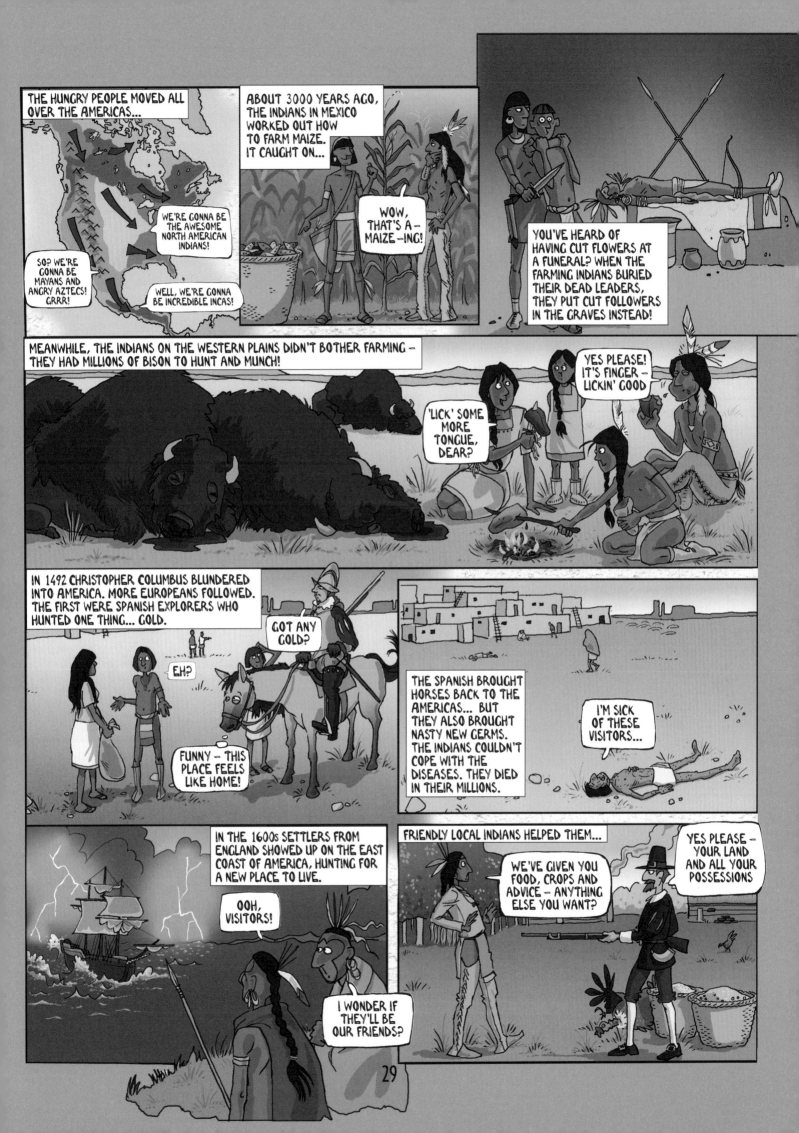

MORE BRITISH SETTLERS KEPT ARRIVING. THE BRITISH GOVERNMENT TRIED TO STOP THEM GRABBING EVEN MORE INDIAN LAND. SO THE SETTLERS SET UP THEIR OWN NATION – THE UNITED STATES OF AMERICA.

WE'RE FREE!

FREE TO GRAB AS MUCH LAND AS WE WANT!

THE NEW U.S. GOVERNMENT DID SIGN SOME TREATIES THAT SAID THE INDIANS COULD KEEP THEIR LAND... BUT THEN THEY BROKE THE TREATIES AND NABBED THE LAND ANYWAY!

THIS RESERVATION HAS NOW BEEN RESERVED FOR US

WE'RE BEING TREATY–D UNFAIRLY

WHEN THE U.S. ARMY TRIED TO PUSH THE SIOUX (SAY SOO) PEOPLE OFF THEIR LAND, THE SIOUX MASSACRED THEM.

THEY WERE HUNTING FOR SOMETHING HORRID – SOLDIERS' SCALPS!

I WISH THEY'D JUST SIOUX–D US

WISELY, THE U.S. GOVERNMENT DECIDED NOT TO FIGHT THE SIOUX ANYMORE. WICKEDLY, THEY DECIDED TO WIPE THEM OUT ANOTHER WAY – BY DESTROYING THEIR FOOD SUPPLY, THE BISON. MILLIONS OF BISON WERE SHOT AND LEFT TO ROT. BEING BEASTLY TO BEASTS HAD BECOME A WAY OF BEING HORRID TO HUMANS.

WHAT A WASTE!

THE SIOUX HAD TO SURRENDER. THEY WERE PUT ON TINY 'RESERVATIONS', JUST LIKE THE OTHER TRIBES. THAT WASN'T THE END OF THEIR WOES...

IN 1890 SOME SOLDIERS WENT TO A SIOUX CAMP AT WOUNDED KNEE TO HUNT DOWN 'TROUBLEMAKERS'. THE SOLDIERS PANICKED AND SHOT DOZENS OF SIOUX MEN, WOMEN AND CHILDREN.

IT WAS A WOUNDED KNEE – JERK REACTION. HARDY HA

NOWADAYS THE INDIANS LIVE AS ORDINARY CITIZENS OR ON THEIR RESERVATIONS. IN SOME RESERVATIONS, INDIANS RUN 'CASINOS' WHERE PEOPLE PLAY GAMBLING CARD GAMES, SUCH AS POKER...

WE WERE ONCE FREE, LIKE POCAHONTAS*

AND NOW YOU'E JUST 'POKER – HUNTERS', RIGHT?

*A FAMOUS INDIAN PRINCESS WHO HELPED SETTLERS.

30

Bison Bits

Here's a Lakota and Cheyenne Indian's guide to getting the best out of the left-over bits (and one bison by-product) of a bison's big body…

Bison bit: GALL BLADDER
Made into: MAKE-UP!
Great for war paint. It'll certainly make you want to fight. You may be yellow-faced but no one will call you call a coward!

Bison bit: SKIN
Used for: you name it!
The tough stuff was used to make teepees, the medium stuff was great for covering balls, the softest stuff was used for top clothes, costumes and berry bags.

Bison bit: DUNG (poo).
Made into: FUEL
Waste not, want not!

Bison bit: TONGUE
Made into: a BRUSH
The hairy side of a bison's tongue could be used to 'lick' your hair into shape. Yuck!

Bison bit: STOMACH
Used as: COOKING POT
Well, more of a cooking bag actually. So the Cheyenne could fill their bellies from a full belly-bag.

Think this bison butchery was gross? Well, the plains Indians did make a right meaty mess… especially once they had guns. But then the white men got bison-bagging. By the 1830s, nearly all the bison east of the Mississippi had been killed by white hunters. Then the government sent the army and hunters to wipe out the bison completely. They couldn't beat the plains Indians in battle, so they had decided to starve them instead. By 1889, the bison were nearly extinct. Woeful for the people who depended on them. Chief Seattle of the Suquamish people said: "What is man without the bison? If all the beasts were gone, men would die from great loneliness of spirit. For whatever happens to the beasts also happens to the man."

Inca-redibly Lousy for Llamas

Down in the place we now call Peru, the ancient Inca people were potty
about sacrificing animals to keep their gods happy...

Incas were the descendants of the Native American Indians who travelled furthest south (see the top of page 29). Just like the Plains Indians, they had a close relationship to the animals that were part of their everyday lives. In the Incas' case it wasn't bison they bashed – it was llamas and guinea pigs!

SQUEAKY SACRIFICES

Do you need a special sacrifice – but are a bit low on dough? Here's a handy hint: save your lovely llama, and sacrifice a guinea pig instead! Yep, these cute little bundles of fur are great for the Inca worshipper on a budget!

Llama harmers

The Incas would sacrifice one hundred llamas every month as part of their religion. (That's a-llama-ing.) One llama, which they named the Napa Llama, was special, though, and wasn't sacrificed. In fact, it was rather pampered. The Inca priests would give it a fancy coat, gold earrings, and lots of beer to drink! (Sounds a bit like a misbehaving monarch!)

DID YOU KNOW?

Incas also asked 'oracles' to tell them the future. The oracle at one bridge was a wooden pole - with big golden bosoms! Maybe it kept them abreast of events?

LLAMA LUNG FUN

Inca priests told the future – by looking at a llama's lungs! Here's how to tell fortunes, Inca style...

FIRST, SACRIFICE A WHITE LLAMA

OPEN ITS CHEST AND PULL OUT ITS LUNGS

BLOW DOWN THE WINDPIPE SO THAT THE LUNGS INFLATE LIKE BALLOONS

THE VEINS WILL STAND OUT. THE PATTERN IN THE VEINS WILL ANSWER YOUR QUESTION

Greedy Soldiers

The history of the British Isles is full of stories of badly behaved guests.
Here is the tale of two Saxon terrors who were paid with land to pop over to do
some chopping – but took a bit more than their host had bargained for...

Hengest and Horsa were the first Saxons to grab a bit of Britain for themselves. But they didn't barge their way in – they were invited!

Rent-a-rabble

After the end of Roman rule in Britain in AD 410, the Britons kept getting invaded by barbarian tribes – especially the Picts (from what we now call Scotland). So Brit leader Vortigern hired some heavy help. He asked Hengest and Horsa, beefy brothers who led a north German tribe, to come over with their warriors to punish the Picts. He offered to pay them with some land.

Pict a spot

The gruesome twosome did their job. The Brits were happy – after all, they weren't getting 'Pict' on anymore. Vortigern was very happy.

Then things started going wrong. Hengest and Horsa demanded a larger lump of land.

Vortigern had to let them have it. (Imagine. You bribe the school bully to stick up for you, and then he demands your dinner money. Not too surprising really, is it?)

Womanly weapon

There was a Brit rebellion against Vortigern, but he just hired Hengest and Horsa to sort it out again. The Saxon siblings brought over twenty more boatloads of their Saxon buddies to help. They also brought a secret weapon – Hengest's daughter!

At a party given by Hengest, Vortigern got a bit gooey. He asked Hengest for his daughter's hand in marriage. Vortigern said, "I will give her anything you want in return!" He meant it, too. Vort said Hengest could have Kent – but it wasn't his to give.

Deadly dining

The Saxons started bashing the Brits and taking more land, but the Brits fought back. So what did horrid Hengest do? He invited Vortigern and his finest men to dinner. But the bullying brothers didn't just carve up the roast – they carved up Vort's men too, and then they threw him in jail. Talk about bad table manners! The Saxons had moved in for good – and for bad.

Lousy Landlords

Here's a scene of lethal landlord behaviour – 'the Clearances' – which took place in the Scottish Highlands in the late 18th century. Life for the Highlanders was tough. When the clan chiefs took up sheep farming, it became un-*baaa*-rable!

HIGHLAND LOWS

1. The Highland clan families lived in simple huts with stone walls and turf roofs. They ate oats, and meat and milk from the cattle they raised. In other words, life was okay if you liked lumpy porridge! But life was about to get lumpier…

2. In the late 18th century, the clan chieftains started to replace their tenants with Lowland sheep farmers (a low trick). The chiefs didn't care two hoots (mon) about the Highlanders.

3. The chiefs wanted to make cash. What they did was to open up all the fields, fill 'em with sheep and sell the wool and mutton. But first they had to turf the Highlanders off their turf.

4. Many Highlanders resisted. (One person even got on the roof to stop the soldiers moving them and fell through – imagine that-ch!)

5. Some Highlanders wouldn't leave their homes. So the buildings were set alight (5A) or knocked down (5B) – while the people were still inside! Char-ming.

6. The men hired by English Lords and Ladies to do the clearing were particularly harsh.

7. The clearers did give the Highlanders a choice: leave and struggle to survive somewhere else in Scotland – or stay and starve. Some choice!

Grim at Glencoe

The Clearances certainly weren't the first bit of brutal behaviour suffered by the Highlanders. In Glencoe, soldiers serving the king did the most dastardly and dishonourable thing a guest can do – murder their hosts.

On 1 February, 1692, 120 troops marched into Glencoe and stayed as guests of the MacDonalds. Two weeks later, those troops murdered 38 MacDonald men, women and children. Hundreds escaped, though many died in the blizzards that swept the bleak mountains. The Highlanders were disgusted. The troops had turned on people who had offered them shelter. And that was something a Highlander just didn't do. The soldiers...

• shot the elderly chief through the head as he called for wine for them to drink
• shot his wife then bit through her fingers to get her rings off
• clubbed, stabbed or shot the MacDonalds as they lay in their beds
• killed a man ill with fever and his five-year-old son, then threw their bodies in the river
• smeared victims' bodies with dung.
They were ordered to kill all 200 people – but they only managed to kill 38. Why?

Tell it to the mountain
Maybe the answer is that many of the soldiers didn't have the heart to do it. Not only did they let 160 escape, they actually warned the MacDonalds the night before the massacre.

One soldier disobeyed orders by saying to his MacDonald hosts, "Let's go for a walk." On the cold mountainside he stopped and started talking to a rock…

GREAT GREY STONE, YOU'VE LIVED HERE SINCE THE BEGINNINGS OF TIME. I'LL BET YOU'VE SEEN SOME STRANGE THINGS, EH? WELL IF YOU KNEW WHAT WAS GOING TO HAPPEN HERE TONIGHT YOU WOULDN'T WANT TO BE HERE TOMORROW MORNING.

Saved by a stone
The MacDonald hosts took the hint and escaped before the massacre. All thanks to a soldier who spoke to a stone. The story is probably true. The stone, known as Henderson's Stone, can be seen in a field at Carnock near Glencoe.

Saxon Sickness

Back in ancient England, the Saxons lived and died with an army of... ailments. Here are four of the foulest!

• **FLEAS** These bloodsuckers cling to clothes tighter than a rottweiler on a burglar's bum. Saxon monks thought that by sealing their habits (robes) in a box, they could suffocate or starve the fleas…

• **LICE** Saxons used combs to pull out the eggs and lice (and hair!). St Cuthbert had a comb made from an elephant's tusk – he must have had jumbo lice!

• **FUNGUS** Old grain goes mouldy with a fungus called ergot. If you make the grain into flour and eat it, you get uncontrollably jerky limbs. In bad cases your toes and fingers turn black and drop off… then you die.

• **WORMS** No, not the sort blackbirds eat. These ones lived inside your body! The monstrous maw-worm could grow to 30 cm and infest your liver or lungs. It could move through your body and pop out anywhere – including the corner of your eye!

PECULIAR PRESCRIPTIONS

Can you match these five foul Saxon ailments to their sick Saxon cures? (Answers on page 61)

AILMENTS	CURES
1 TOOTHACHE	A. BEAT YOURSELF WITH A WHIP MADE FROM A DOLPHIN'S SKIN.
2 SWOLLEN EYELID	B. BOIL A HOLLY LEAF, LAY IT ON A SAUCER OF WATER, RAISE IT TO THE MOUTH AND YAWN.
3 SICK GIRL	C. CUT THE SIGN OF THE CROSS IN THE FOREHEAD, BACK AND LIMBS, PIERCE THE LEFT EAR, THEN BEAT WITH A STICK.
4 MADNESS	D. CUT A VEIN AND LET OUT SOME BLOOD. THIS MUST BE DONE AT NIGHT.
5 SICK HORSE	E. TAKE A KNIFE AND CUT OUT THE AFFECTED PART.

Here's a Saxon cure for headaches that was also said to scare off goblins! Put stones from swallow chicks' stomachs on your head. No goblins around? It must have worked well, then!

DAFT DEEDS

Rotten Remedies

Of course, Saxon times were a long time ago, so you'd expect them to have some odd ideas.
But centuries later, in Georgian times, the doctors were still quite crackers!

The Georgians didn't quite understand how the human body worked. Doctors often made their patients feel worse than before. And dentists weren't much better.

Pukey potions

Newspapers were packed with adverts for curious cures. Here are just three potions on sale that sold like hot – err – medicines:
• **Mallow flowers and squashed snail mix.** Perfect for shivering fevers. (Would you rather have the shakes?)
• **Sugar, nutmeg and woodlouse powder.** Mix with wee and drink – to stop cancer. (Sounds lousy.)
• **Squashed fish eyes.** Guaranteed to relieve toothache. (Eye eye!) Not to mention dung tea, stewed owls and crushed worms…

Dental dread

Scared of the dentist? Count yourself lucky you weren't a Georgian with a jaw pain! To treat a bad tooth, the dentist tied you down and ripped it out. But here's the gummily gross bit… If you were rich, he might have a child lie beside you. As soon as the dentist had torn out your bad tooth, he'd rip a good 'live' tooth from the kid – and push it in the gap in your gums! (Don't worry, the child got paid!) Sometimes, instead of children's teeth, the extracted or missing gnashers were replaced with false ones made from hippo or walrus tusks.

Corpses for cash

Georgian doctors saw that the only way to learn more about the body's mysteries was to cut one up. But where could they get bodies to practise on? The gallows, of course! So surgeons were allowed to cut up the cadavers (dead bodies) of hanged criminals.

Amazingly, even with all those hangings, there weren't enough cadavers to go around. This was where 'bodysnatchers' came in. They dug up freshly buried corpses from graveyards and sold them to the surgeons. The surgeons paid well and asked no questions.

Scary Hare and bloody Burke

William Burke and William Hare are the most famous bodysnatchers. But these two Edinburgh ghouls didn't snatch dead bodies… they made their own! The deadly duo had a sinister scheme. They gave gave homeless people a cheap room for the night – and then killed them. Burke and Hare sold the freshly slaughtered bodies to a surgeon.

The wicked Williams were caught in 1828. Burke was hanged… and then his body was cut up by curious doctors. Bet after that he wished he 'cad-a-ver' proper funeral (groan!).

COLLECTION OF CURIOUS CURES

Seven Georgian cures you should never try... or rather, six.
But which one is the phoney Georgian fix?

1. Sty on your eyelid? Rub it with the tail of a black cat. (Don't really – it's NOT a good eye-dea!)

2. Painful, swollen joints? Try this cure insisted on by a man called Thomas Grey. Boil a whole chicken and wash it down with six litres of beer. Grey said 'a friend' tried it and it worked. (More like he got drunk and tried to cover it up...)

3. People bitten by a mad dog could catch rabies. One cure was to take a bath in salt water. A bitten man from Bristol was taken for a dip in the sea. When they hauled him back into the boat, he immediately died. This cure never worked.

4. For toothache, the Georgians took a poker and heated it in a fire. When it was nice and hot, they burned the ear lobe with the poker. YOW!

5. Boil on the bum? The idea was to burst it quickly. A kick from a horse was the Georgian way for a very quick burst.

6. Rotten teeth gave the Georgians terrible breath. They believed the best cure was to scrape the skin off a turnip, roast the pieces and wear them behind the ears. Well, at least the stink of turnip meant you didn't notice the whiffy breath!

7. An adder bite is nasty... but the Georgian cure was nastier! In 1821 a woman was bitten by an adder near Southampton. The local people killed a chicken and placed its warm guts over the wound. Talk about 'fowl'!

BEDLAM, HOME OF HORRORS

1. Roll up, roll up! There was always a queue to get in.
2. Inside, the gawping crowds saw some sorry sights. Some poor patients were left in their own filth (2A) and just had to fight for whatever food they were given (2B).
3. Nurses would sometimes whip patients – either as punishment or to put on a shocking show for the vile visitors.
4. Mad people were seen as a trendy accessory. If you had the cash, you could hire a loony to laugh at for your party!
5. Visitors stared at a woman who had been chained to a wall. Her cell was riddled with rats.
6. The treatments the patients were given were awful. They were forced to drink mercury (6A), a poison that would make your gums bled and your teeth fall out. If you weren't a bit batty already, the mercury would make you quite mad, too (6B)!
7. One woman who had fits was drenched with buckets of freezing water. Chilling.
8. Doctors bled patients to relieve their madness. It just made them weaker, of course.
9. There was one good thing about having nosey ninnys poking round the hospital – it meant the nurses had to behave themselves! When the public weren't around, they would really 'try' their patients.

Mean for the Mad

It wasn't just the mentally ill poor who were treated terribly...

London's Bethlehem Hospital (Bedlam for short) was just one place where ordinary people who became mentally ill would be locked away. Sadly, your treatment wasn't much better if you were posh – or even a slightly crackers king!

Goofy George III

George III is famous for being bonkers, even though he was only mentally ill for short periods. (He had some crackpot ideas when he was 'normal', too, such as insisting that Catholics shouldn't be allowed to vote.) When he was ill, he couldn't rule a line, never mind a country. At different times, George…

• 'Adopted' a baby that he called Prince Octavius… who was actually a pillow.

• Ended each sentence with the word 'peacock'. He once opened Parliament by saying: "My Lords and peacocks…"

• Believed that London was flooded and ordered a yacht.

• Believed he was dead, so he wore black in mourning for "that good man, George III".

Crackpot king cures

George's doctors did their very best – or worst! – to cure George. Their so-called treatments included…

• Fastening him to his bed.

• Shouting at him – after stuffing handkerchiefs in his mouth so that he couldn't answer back.

• Forming blisters on his head then bursting them – to let the 'badness' out of his head.

Some Georgian folk were so rich and silly they actual PAID for utterly potty 'health treatments' even when they weren't actually sick. (Although maybe this proves they were a bit batty.) There were plenty of 'quacks' – doctors with dotty ideas – to take advantage of their stupidity and their money. Take James Graham. He opened a posh 'Temple of Health' in London, where foolish rich people paid huge sums of money for his hare-brained health treatments.

These included...
• Being buried up to the neck in a bath of earth.
• Sitting in a bed filled with magnets and horsehair.
In the end Graham went barmy. He wore a suit made of grass, invented a new religion and wrote a book called How to Live for Many Weeks or Months Without Eating Anything Whatsoever. He followed the diet to his dying day... which came very soon.

Factory Facts... or Fibs?

In Victorian times, Britain was the boss of the world when it came to making stuff. (It helped that Britain had made itself boss of most of the world, too... but that's another story.) Making stuff means factories, and factories mean... meanness.

Here are ten statements about vile Victorian factory life. But which are terribly true and which are fiendishly false?

1 You weren't allowed to breathe between the hours of 9am and 5pm.

2 There was a fine for whistling or singing while you worked.

3 You started work at 6am, but breakfast wasn't until 8am.

4 There was a rule against losing fingers in the machinery.

5 You were fined for talking with anyone in another department.

6 Anyone dying at work would be sacked at once.

7 The managers would alter the clocks so you'd be late for work, then they'd fine you for your lateness.

8 No young children were to be brought by parents into the factory.

9 'Mould runners' (child workers in the Midland potteries) worked for 12 hours in temperatures of up to 40°C (120°F).

10 Boy labourers worked for chain-smiths and used huge hammers. This helped make them tough and strong.

Invention Century

The Victorian age was chock-a-block with change – some of it super and splendid, some of it savage and strange! Here's how Britain become faster and nastier...

OTHER INVENTIONS WERE AWFUL IN A DIFFERENT WAY. THE MACHINE-GUN MADE IT EASY TO MASSACRE PEOPLE ALL OVER THE WORLD. THIS HELPED THE BRITS TO BUILD A MIGHTY EMPIRE.

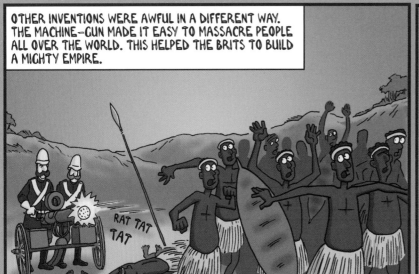

RAT TAT TAT

BRITAIN MAY HAVE BEEN THE RICHEST COUNTRY IN THE WORLD, BUT LIFE FOR MOST FOLKS IN ITS CITIES WAS STILL HORRIBLY POOR. MOST HOUSES HAD NO SEWAGE SYSTEMS. DRINKING WATER WAS OFTEN POLLUTED WITH HUMAN POO, SO PEOPLE DIED OF DEADLY DISEASES SUCH AS CHOLERA.

COME ON SON — IF IT'S BROWN, DRINK IT DOWN!

SOME VICTORIANS SET THEIR MINDS TO SORTING THIS OUT. SEWERS AND FRESH WATER SUPPLIES WERE BUILT, SO THE CITIES BECAME HEALTHIER PLACES.

YUCK! THIS 'FRESH' WATER AIN'T GOT NO FLAVOUR!

WRITERS SUCH AS CHARLES DICKENS WROTE STORIES ABOUT HOW WOEFUL LIFE HAD BEEN FOR WORKERS — ESPECIALLY CHILDREN.

SHUSH, HE'S READING!

IT'S HORRIBLE HOW THOSE CHILD WORKERS SUFFER

EXCUSE ME, MA'AM, COULD YOU PUT THE FIRE OUT?

MANY WELL-OFF PEOPLE WERE SHOCKED AND DID THEIR BIT TO MAKE THINGS BETTER.

LAWS WERE PASSED TO MAKE LIFE LESS LOUSY FOR FACTORY WORKERS, TO STOP CHILDREN HAVING TO WORK IN FACTORIES — AND TO GIVE THE KIDS AN EDUCATION.

HURRAH!

BOO! I BET WE HAVE TO GO TO SCHOOL INSTEAD

GOOD NEWS CHILDREN! YOU DON'T HAVE TO WORK IN FACTORIES ANYMORE!

THE VICTORIANS TRIED TO CREATE A WORLD OF FAST TRAVEL, WORLDWIDE COMMUNICATIONS, BIG BUSINESS AND TOP TECHNOLOGY — BUT ENDED UP HAVING TERRIBLE TROUBLES ON THE WAY. (SOUND FAMILIAR?)

Dire Drains

Factory filth wasn't the only kind of dirt that could ruin an early-Victorian's day... and life. The sewers were deadly, too – and leaking lethal poo!

L et's face it – once you've pulled the chain, you don't want to see what you've done again. But some Victorians had to drink it and wash in it!

Four foul sewage statistics

1 Proper drains weren't built in London until 1865. Before then the waste from sinks and toilets ran down old sewers into the River Thames – or drained into huge cesspools under houses. It wasn't just people's poo that was a problem either. 1000 tonnes of horse manure dropped onto the streets of London each day. Every big street had a crossing lady who, for a penny, would sweep the street in front of you as you crossed.

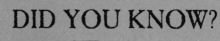

A HORSE HAS BEATEN YOU TO IT, MA'AM

LOOKS LIKE I'LL HAVE TO SPEND A PENNY

2 Until the mid-1860s, London relied on water pumped from the River Thames as its main source of water. But up to 200 sewers emptied into it! Raw sewage could be seen coming out of standpipes in the streets of London. And even in posh houses with running water, the water flowed a 'healthy' brown colour!

AREN'T YOU GOING TO FLUSH THE LOO, MASTER THOMAS?

I JUST DID

In London in 1847, an inspector discovered that sewage was a problem which would not go away on its own. He reported…

The filth was lying scattered around the rooms, vaults, cellars and yards, so thick and so deep, that it was hardly possible to move around it.

3 In 1852 a small room was opened, just for men, in Fleet Street. They were very relieved… it was the first flushing public toilet. There wasn't one for women – they just had to keep their legs crossed!

FIRST PUBLIC FLUSHING TOILET

I THOUGHT PEE CAME BEFORE QUEUE?

DID YOU KNOW?

In 1884 a lady wrote that people were pleased when they smelled bad drains. Why? It was a sign of bad weather on the way. People were glad of the warning, even though it was a bit whiffy.

AND THE FORECAST FOR TODAY... STINKS!

4 The Victorian poor were known as 'The Great Unwashed'. That's because poorer

WHAT ARE THOSE PIECES OF PAPER FLOATING DOWN THE RIVER?

THOSE MADAM, ARE NOTICES SAYING THAT BATHING IS FORBIDDEN

areas of towns had to get their water from standpipes in the street. There was barely enough to cook with, let alone wash.

What's in the water?

Today's tap water is clean enough to drink. But what was in Victorian water…?

Cash London 'toshers' waded through sewage every day – up to 1.5 metres deep in the gloop. Why? They were looking for coins and other useful metal stuff dropped through the drains. Would you stick your hand down an unflushed toilet for your pocket money? Toshers would. (And that's what people mean when they say "What a lot of tosh!")

Bodies Some men had the job of clearing rubbish from the River Thames… and of recovering dead bodies. There was a reward for finding a missing person, but the Thames body-finders had an extra reward – they stripped the body of its valuables. As Charles Dickens wrote:

Has a dead body any use for money? Is it possible for a dead man to have money? Can a corpse own it, want it, spend it, claim it, miss it?

Paper It wasn't just London that stank like a loo. There was a similarly smelly situation in Cambridge. All the sewage flowed into the Cam (Cambridge's river), which made it pretty disgusting to walk beside. In 1843, Queen Victoria was walking beside the river when she asked a university teacher an embarrassing question. She had seen bits of poo-covered toilet paper floating on the water and she wanted to know what they were. Unlikely as it sounds, this teacher came up with a pretty smart answer.

Cholera In 1831 a new import arrived… a beastly germ called cholera (say coller-ra). Cholera gives you disgusting diarrhoea, turns you blue and kills you. It killed 20,000 people in the following year. How does cholera spread? By being carried from sufferers' sewage into the water supply. And guess what? That's what happened. London's dire drains helped it out. They carried cholera-packed poo straight into the Thames, which people drank, which gave them cholera, which got into the drains. In 1853 cholera killed 11,500 people in London alone.

Foul Facts

One summer, the Thames got so thick with sewage that it barely flowed at all. It was the summer of 1858. To make matters worse, it was a particularly hot summer too. So it's no wonder that Londoners called it the summer of the 'Great Stink'.
The blinds of the Houses of Parliament had to be soaked in chloride of lime so that the MPs could meet without choking on the smell. In the end the smell got so bad they decided to take an early break.

GENTLEBEN, PLEASE! THIS IS HER BAJESTY'S HOUSE OF COBBONS!

ODOUR, ODOUR!

THESE MOTIONS HAVE BEEN PASSED!

Jobs and Snobs

In Victorian times, being a servant was one way to earn a reasonable living. There were rotten rules to obey and lots of silly snobbery. Here's your guide to a rich household's servants – who to rub up the right way and who to snootily snub...

UPPER SERVANTS

Valet
Dresses and shaves his master, irons his newspaper. (Let's hope he doesn't get the two mixed up!)

Cook
Cooks and bosses around the kitchen maids and scullery maid.

Butler
Announces visitors, minds the wine cellar. He's the top servant – and never lets the others forget it!

Housekeeper
Minds the house linen and candles, makes life miserable for the housemaids. You could almost say she has it 'maid'.

Lady's maid
Makes sure the lady of the house looks fabulous. Not always an easy job!

LOWER SERVANTS

Nursemaid
Takes care of the family's bratty sprogs!

Housemaid
Dusts, polishes, cleans, lights fires, carries coal and water, empties the family's potties!

Footmen
Nice but dim. They stand around looking good in silk stockings and powdered wigs. They think they're the bee's knees.

Kitchen maid
Peels spuds, gets shouted at. Like the potatoes, she gets a real roasting from the cook.

Scullery maid
Scrubs the gunge off pans until her hands are red-raw and blistered.

52

A day in the life of a parlour-maid...

...or 'Is it worth going to bed?' In poorer households, parlour-maids had to do all the housework themselves! Here's a typical schedule...

A.M

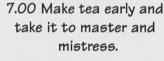

10.30
Go to bed.
Next day... start all over again.
Of course, you would be paid. Paid nearly six pounds – six pounds a YEAR that is!

6.00
Get out of bed, wash, dress, brush hair into a bun.

6.30
Go downstairs. Put the kettle on. Pull up blinds, open windows, clean fireplaces.

10.00
Eat own supper, wash up.

8.30
Clear dinner table, wash up.

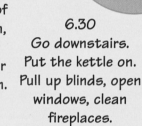

7.00 Make tea early and take it to master and mistress.

7.30 Sweep the dining room and dust. Lay the table for breakfast.

7.00
Serve dinner and wait at table.

8.00 Serve breakfast.

6.00
Lay the table for dinner.

1.00 Eat own lunch, then do laundry or clean all the carpets.

12.00 Change dress to serve lunch; lay the lunch table, serve the lunch, clear the table, wash up all the glass and silver, put everything away in its place.

9.00 Clear breakfast table, wash up, put on clean apron, make the beds, clean the taps, wash the baths and bathroom floors, clean the toilets, dust every bedroom.

8.30 Go upstairs, strip the beds, open the bedroom windows, have own breakfast.

P.M

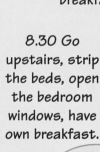

English Aggro

Think the English are a peaceful lot? Think again! English history is peppered with riots, revolts and plots. Here's what happens the English get aggravated...

THE ENGLISH HATE PEOPLE TELLING THEM WHAT TO DO. NOT SURPRISINGLY THERE HAVE BEEN RIOTS RIGHT THROUGH ENGLAND'S HISTORY...

OKAY, HISTORY'S OVER, YOU CAN STOP RIOTING NOW

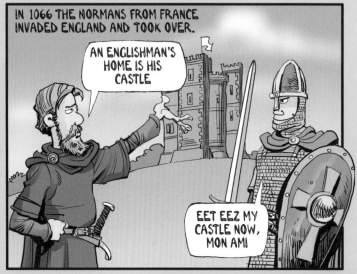

IN 1066 THE NORMANS FROM FRANCE INVADED ENGLAND AND TOOK OVER.

AN ENGLISHMAN'S HOME IS HIS CASTLE

EET EEZ MY CASTLE NOW, MON AMI

THE NORMANS INTRODUCED THE FEUDAL SYSTEM...

WE CALL IT THE FEUDAL SYSTEM BECAUSE THEY GROW THE 'FEUD'...

...AND WE EAT IT. HA HA!

I'LL GIVE YOU 'FEUD' FOR THOUGHT...

IN THE MIDDLE AGES, SOME PEASANTS REBELLED – QUIETLY! IN 1381, KING RICHARD II TRIED TO MAKE THE PEASANTS PAY EXTRA TAX, SO LOTS OF FAMILIES 'DISAPPEARED'.

PLAGUE, MATE

THEY CAN'T ALL HAVE DIED SINCE LAST YEAR

CAN I GET UP YET MUMMY?

OTHERS WEREN'T SO PEACEFUL. WAT TYLER LED A NOISY REBELLION AGAINST TAX COLLECTORS. RICHARD HAD TYLER'S HEAD STUCK ON A POLE. NO WONDER NO ONE WANTED WAT'S JOB!

THERE'S A VACANT POST FOR ANYONE WHO WANTS IT

THE MIDDLE AGES WERE PRETTY MISERABLE. SO YOU'D THINK PEOPLE WOULD BE GLAD WHEN THEY CAME TO AN END.

MID'L AGES

GOOD RIDDANCE

BUT THE TUDOR AND STUART TIMES THAT FOLLOWED WERE WORSE. YOU COULD GET TORTURED OR EXECUTED – JUST FOR HAVING THE 'WRONG' RELIGION.

WAIT, COME BACK!

SO WHICH WAS THE RIGHT RELIGION? THE KING'S OR QUEEN'S, OF COURSE! THE ONLY TROUBLE WAS THEY KEPT SWAPPING BETWEEN BEING CATHOLIC AND PROTESTANT – AND SOME WERE BOTH. YOU JUST COULDN'T KEEP UP – WHICH MEANT LOTS OF TRADE FOR TORTURERS...

TORTURE TOOLS 'Я' US

I'VE A GOOD FEELING ABOUT OUR NEW BUSINESS

PART OF THE PROBLEM WAS THAT ENGLAND NEVER SEEMED TO HAVE ENGLISH KINGS. HENRY VI WAS WELSH. JAMES VI OF SCOTLAND CAME DOWN TO LONDON TO BE JAMES I OF ENGLAND.

THERE'S SOMETHING WRITTEN ON THE CROWN – 'FOREIGN FOREHEADS FOREVER'!

NOT SURPRISINGLY, PEOPLE GOT FED UP. SOME EVEN PLOTTED TO BLOW UP THEIR RULERS – WITH GUNPOWDER.

THE FIFTH? BUT THAT'S FIREWORKS NIGHT!

THAT PLOT WAS A FLOP, BUT OTHER PLOTS TURNED OUT TO BE NONSENSE...

..THE 'POPISH PLOT' OF 1678 FOR ONE. THE ANTI-CATHOLIC PROTESTER TITUS OATES MADE UP A TALE ABOUT ENGLAND BEING INVADED BY A FRENCH (CATHOLIC) ARMY OUT TO KILL KING CHARLES II. PEOPLE IN DORSET FLED THE COAST IN TERROR. THEY SCREAMED...

THE FRENCH HAVE LANDED!

BUT NEXT MORNING, WHEN THE SUN ROSE...

SORRY – JUST A HEDGE. EASY MISTAKE TO MAKE.

MANY INNOCENT CATHOLICS WERE TORTURED AND EXECUTED BECAUSE OF TITUS OATES.

AS WELL AS BEING PLOT POTTY, ANOTHER TYPICAL ENGLISH ATTITUDE IS BEING BLOODY-MINDED. WHEN A NOTICE WAS SENT TO JAIL TELLING PHILIP EVANS HE'D BEEN SENTENCED TO DIE, HE KNEW WHAT WAS GOING TO HAPPEN – BUT INSTEAD OF PANICKING, HE SAID TO THE MESSENGER...

CAN'T READ IT NOW OLD CHAP. I WANT TO FINISH MY GAME OF TENNIS FIRST

WHILE HE WAITED TO BE HANGED, EVANS CALMLY PLAYED THE HARP IN HIS CELL. (PLUCKY OR WHAT?)

IN FACT, MANY ENGLISH HEROES ARE FAMOUS FOR BEING PIG-HEADED. TAKE ADMIRAL NELSON. AT THE BATTLE OF COPENHAGEN, ONE OF HIS SHIPS SIGNALLED TO HIM TO RETREAT. NELSON WANTED TO FINISH THE BATTLE SO HE PUT HIS TELESCOPE TO HIS BAD EYE AND SAID...

I have only one eye, I have a right to be blind sometimes. I really do not see the signal!

BUT BACK TO THE REBELLIONS. TOFFS COULD BE REBELLIOUS TOO! IN 1780 LORD GORDON LED A MARCH TO PARLIAMENT AGAINST CATHOLICS. HIS MOB ATTACKED CHAPELS, PRISONS AND HOUSES. ABOUT 700 PEOPLE DIED IN THE 'GORDON RIOTS'.

GORDON RIOTS!

DEAR ME, DOES HE?

IN VICTORIAN TIMES, ENGLAND WAS FULL OF FACTORIES POWERED BY NEW MACHINES. NO REASON TO PROTEST AGAINST MACHINES – THEY MADE LIFE EASIER FOR THE WORKERS, RIGHT?

OR WE HAVE TO FIND JOBS WITH LONG HOURS AND VERY LITTLE MONEY, WE'RE EXHAUSTED

NO, ACTUALLY. IF MACHINES DO OUR WORK WE ARE OUT OF A JOB. WE'RE STARVING

I'M EXHAUSTED AND STARVING

SMASH THE ROTTEN MACHINES!

THESE DAYS THE WORLD IS FULL OF MEAN MACHINES CALLED 'NUCLEAR MISSILES'. NO REASON TO PROTEST AGAINST WAR MACHINES – THEY'LL MAKE FIGHTING WARS EASIER AND MAKE US FEEL SAFER, RIGHT?

NO MORE WAR

NO WAY!

BAN THE BOMB

NO

SMASH THE ROTTEN MACHINES!

IT SEEMS THAT, IN ENGLAND, IF YOU REALLY WANT TO CHANGE THINGS, YOU HAVE TO MAKE A NUISANCE OF YOURSELF. WHEN WOMEN TRIED TO GET THE VOTE IN THE EARLY 20TH CENTURY, THEY HAD TO DO SOME PRETTY EXTREME THINGS BEFORE PEOPLE LISTENED.

WELL IF YOU PUT IT LIKE THAT...

IN 1989 THE 'PEASANTS' REVOLTED AGAIN – WHEN PRIME MINISTER MARGARET THATCHER TRIED TO BRING BACK THE POLL TAX! IN THE END THEY MADE HER BACK DOWN, AND SHE LOST HER JOB.

I WISH I COULD PUT THOSE PEASANTS' HEADS ON POLES!

Rebel or Rubbish?

Legendary leader of the ancient Britons, King Arthur is supposed to rise from his grave to fight off trouble if anyone should try to bully the Brits. The trouble is he would be a bit mouldy... and he might not have even existed!

Stories tell about a leader of the Britons who battled the Saxons and won forty years of peace. His name was 'Arthur'. Now, there are all kinds of stories floating around about this hero. Take your pick...

THE GREAT ARTHUR DEBATE

BRAVE RESPECTED HERO	GREEDY CRUEL VILLAIN	NOBLE GOD-FEARING KNIGHT	STORY-BOOK LEGEND
BRITISH MONK AD 540	WELSH POET AD 1000	NORMAN MONK AD 1300	HISTORIAN AD 2000

Camelot of nonsense

Poets from the Middle Ages will tell you that Arthur pulled a sword out of a stone, lived in a posh castle called Camelot, and rushed all over the place in a suit of gleaming armour, leading the Knights of the Round Table in a quest to find the Holy Grail. That's all poetic piffle, of course. However, Arthur may really have existed. Some historians think he was a leader of a travelling band of Celtic warriors who fought against Saxon invaders in the

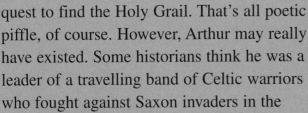

5th century. The trouble is no one wrote about him until 300 years after his death, so it could be Celtic claptrap after all.

I PREFERRED THE OTHER COSTUME

Merlin – magic or tragic?

Think King Arthur's famous wizard sidekick was made up? Think again. Merlin – or Myrddin – really did exist. What do we know about him? Not a lot. He was...

• *a Welsh 'bard' – that's a singing poet. (So not very likely to help the English, then, is he?)*

• *He went a bit bonkers after fighting in a battle in AD 573. And that's it! Of course, the legends are more interesting...*

Magical mover

According to ancient tales, Merlin wasn't just a punchy poet – he was also a kind of dynamic delivery man. Amazing Merlin was the one who brought the stones for Stonehenge all the way from Ireland to Salisbury in England. How did he carry them? Ropes? Horses? A lorry? No. He used magic. Handy!

STONES TO GO – WITH EXTRA TOPPING

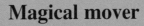

Woe for Welsh Workers

Here are some Welsh rioters who were DEFINITELY real. In 1831, the iron-making town of Merthyr Tydfil in South Wales was the scene of a rotten riot – and an even more ruthless reaction...

A TRUNKFUL OF TROUBLE

1. The selfish ironworks bosses started the trouble by cutting 84 people's jobs, lowering the wages of the rest. They also treated those in debt terribly, by taking their things as payment. 10,000 furious local folk marched into town.

2. At the front was Lewis Lewis. He lost his temper after bailiffs took away a trunk belonging to him in payment for a debt. Lewis was more used to hunting foxes than bosses – but he still wanted blood!

3. The High Sheriff of Glamorgan told them to clear off. They wouldn't, so he really read the Riot Act – twice!

4. A church minister, the Reverend David John, was there to 'rev up' the wild workers.

5. They gathered outside the Castle Inn, waving a revolting flag – a white sheet soaked in calves' blood ('blood of the workers'). The pole had a loaf of bread on top. (What was that? The 'butty of the workers'?) They demanded an end to the courts taking their stuff, a decent wage – and an MP in Parliament. Sounds fair? That's not what the bosses thought.

6. Ironmaster William Crawshay told the crowd to calm down, saying he was on their side. Did it work? Of course not!

7. 'Special' constables (part-time policeman) didn't have the nerve for the fight. They ran away. Not very 'special' then!

8. The crowd threw stones, and waved axes, clubs and pitchforks…

9. …but the soldiers fired their guns.

10. 70 workers were injured. 24 were killed.

11. If they weren't 'clocked', rioters took the chance to take back their property.

ANSWERS

Terrify Your Teacher (page 8)

1c) Stone Age artists may have also used animal fats.

2a) If you said "Hedgehog skin" then you deserve to try it!

3c) They sprinkled spare spuds with water and left them out at night to freeze.

4a) So there's no excuse!

5a) One professor thinks Stone Age folks threw pottery figures into fires to make them explode.

Fireside Frights (page 13)

The correct answer to every question is c).

If you have picked just one a) or b), you've probably bought yourself a ticket to the Otherworld!

1c) The Celts drank small sips... but drank an awful lot of them!

2c) Warriors took part in boasting contests. Exaggerating was all part of the fun.

3c) Warriors ate only the best meat.

4c) Druids knew that mistletoe was a poison – after all, they gave it to sacrificial victims. (You can see them cutting it in the Grim Grove on pages 10–11.)

Riddle Muddle (page 13)

Did you get stuck? Don't worry. It was designed to leave Celts clueless, too. Here's the solution...

A woman (two legs) comes in carrying a leg of lamb (one leg) and puts it down on a stool (three legs). A dog (four legs) comes in and runs off with it. You can work out the rest from there!

Brutal for Bulls (page 24)

b). People drank far too much and went absolutely wild. No one cared about the bulls!

Frost Fair (page 14-15)

Royal Rotters ... and Rats! (page 20)

1. Edward the Confessor. 2. Harold. 3. William the Conqueror. 4. Henry I. 5. Stephen. 6. Matilda. 7. Richard the Lionheart. 8. John. 9 . Edward II. 10. Henry IV. 11. Henry V. 12. Henry VI. 13. Edward V. 14. Richard III. 15. Henry VIII. 16. Edward VI. 17. Mary I. 18. Elizabeth I. 19. James I. 20. Charles I. 2. Charles I. 22. James II. 23. Mary II. 24. William III. 25. George III. 26. William IV. 7. Victoria. 28. Edward VII. 29. Elizabeth II.
The rats are ringed below...

Peculiar Prescriptions (page 29)

1b) 'Evil toothworms will tumble from the mouth'. Yuck! 2e) A Saxon book says that a youth survived a knife through the eyelid. 3d). 4a) You may not be mad after the whipping, but the dolphin would be furious. 5c) So it makes the horse a little cross!

Collection of Curious Cures (page 41)

5) is the phoney. Georgians weren't quite barmy enough to let their boily bottoms be booted by horses.

Factory Facts ... or Fibs? (page 45)

1. False. 2. True. 3. True 4. False. 5. True 6. False 7. True. 8. False. (Have a look in the mill on pages 48-49.) 9. True. 10. False – their frail bodies were crippled for life.

PICTURE CREDITS

5 Martin Brown; 6-7 Robin Carter; 8 Martin Brown;
9 Martin Brown; 10-11 Patrice Aggs; 12 Martin
Brown; 13 Gary Northfield; 14-15 Leo Hartas; 16
Christyan Fox (l) Gary Northfield (tr, br); 17-19 Dave
Shelton; 20 Kate Sheppard; 21 Dave Shelton; 22-23
Patrice Aggs; 24-25 Martin Brown; 26-27 Patrice
Aggs; 28-30 Geri Ford; 31 Clive Spong; 32 Chantal
Kees; 33 Martin Brown (l, bl), Gary Northfield (r);
34-35 Patrice Aggs; 36-37 Geri Ford; 38 Martin
Brown; 39 Martin Brown; 40-41 Martin Brown; 42-43
Patrice Aggs; 44 Gary Northfield (l, b) Martin Brown
(r); 45 Martin Brown; 46-47 Dave Shelton;48-49
Patrice Aggs; 50 -51 Martin Brown, Chantal Kees; 52
Dave Shelton; 53 Martin Brown; 54-56 Kev Hopgood;
57 Martin Brown (tl, l), Dave Shelton (r, br); 58-59
Patrice Aggs.